CW01160325

Copyright © 2020 by Ania Epul.

Library of Congress Control Number:		2020907074
ISBN:	Hardcover	978-1-7960-9827-3
	Softcover	978-1-7960-9826-6
	eBook	978-1-7960-9861-7

All rights reserved. No part of this book may be reproduced or transmitted in any form or by any means, electronic or mechanical, including photocopying, recording, or by any information storage and retrieval system, without permission in writing from the copyright owner.

Any people depicted in stock imagery provided by Getty Images are models, and such images are being used for illustrative purposes only. Certain stock imagery © Getty Images.

Print information available on the last page.

Rev. date: 04/22/2020

To order additional copies of this book, contact:
Xlibris
1-888-795-4274
www.Xlibris.com
Orders@Xlibris.com
811893

WITHIN THESE WALLS

ANIA EPUL

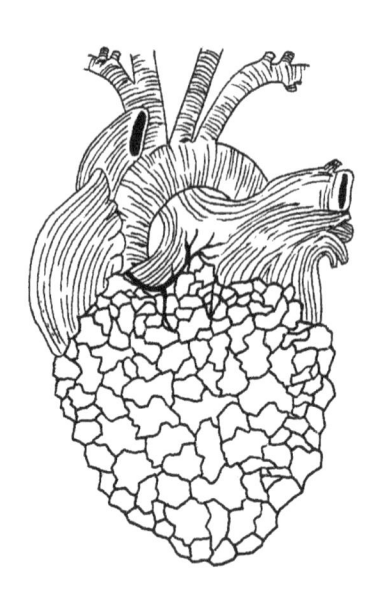

ania epul

a smile
turned frown
the corners of lips
turned down

when truth
earns no earnest,
the earnest
smear lies over honesty

alive, there is chaos,
the frostbite of cruelty,
and charred hearts turn hard
beneath stars

~ metamorphoses

within these walls

a stranger among every colony,
living alone in a world
covered in an eternity of nothingness

defined under the shadow
of so many scintillating stars,
under too many barely healed scars,
under the shadow of fistfuls of torn dreams

my hopes to become had long sunken

the streams ran dry,
and there were no boats to carry them

dulled in a sea of a million others,
nothing but a drop of water in the sea

nothing
but another weed too short to be the stars,
and too tall to rest against the soils

but everyone keeps going where they're going,
and you're only a sideshow

you think they're coming toward you,
but they're stepping around you,
pushing past you

you think they're here to talk
when they stop,
but they're only asking for directions
to their next destination

within these walls

you dream to be everything
for everyone
everywhere
for all time

but you can't.

if you want to be something absolute,
all you can be is

NOTHING

show's over.
curtains drawn
and i am nothing

no one more to bullshit
no more laughs to extract from people's voice boxes
no more tears to wring out of people's tear ducts

.

now what?

i'm tired from the show.

i wipe off the clown makeup
slick the lies from my mouth
roll up the backdrop
pop the balloons
      (i deflate with them)

we sink to the floor.
we are tired.

i see my reflection in the metallic stage

who are you?
      who *are* you, you stranger!

within these walls

tomato wedge
feelingless parabola
i wish i could feel something
but what would i feel?

i wish i could feel something

good.

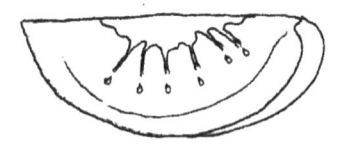

abandoned by a hundred smiles
ignoring a thousand opportunities gathering dust
whiling away a million hours flitting past
dull in the face of a billion creativities
idle in the wake of so many moments trampling me

sleeping through another day.

~ anhedonic treadmill

within these walls

if i'm not sitting staring at the wall,
then i'm lying
        staring at the ceiling

i'm starting to wonder
if these arms and legs even belong to me

where is this coming from
where is my mind

maybe i'm not real
does today even exist

i have to go somewhere,
but where do i go

i can't just keep getting up and leaving,
but i'm on autopilot so i just keep on going

the question is
where am i going?
        and when does this end??

this.

last time someone tugged some emotion out of my
cotton-nothing-insides
was when they mentioned

this.

before that, i felt nothing.
i thought nothing.
i was nothing.
my entire life revolves around

this.

the only thing i think about

is this.

i have to change.
i can't change.
i have to tell someone.
i am guarding this secret with my life and everything my life
can buy.

i always think i've lost the ability to feel anything,
and i genuinely wonder if i will ever feel anything again,
but then someone brings up

this.

and then suddenly i feel

within these walls

eVeRyThInG ! ! !

until i lie my way out
and fit myself back into the container,
and then i close my eyes
     and take a deep breath
          and everything goes away
              and the hole in me grows.

~ crescit eundo

drill at my temples
skull nailed to the pillow
sheep in the ceiling

can't think with this bleating in my brain
can't move with this wool in my limbs
i can't
i. can't.
i can't do ANYTHING

~ how am i supposed to?

within these walls

how many more
minutes before i can finally say that it's all over?

how many more
breaths will i struggle to breathe before i'm freed?

how many more
memories will i live through
just so they can make tomorrow harder to live through?

how many more mistakes will i make?
wrong turns will i take??
nights will i spend lying awake???

~ how many more?

ania epul

the nearby eyes
bicker and smile
wreathed in grime
crave to defile

reword the wires
suffocate the sockets
when sparks don't fly,
ignite the fires

blind lights blinking
guts are sinking
the black forked tongue
flicks from the waves

the bound coils snap
to an openmouthed gape…
it pours ink like syrup—
ink on the mind of a child.

ania epul

kaleidoscope daisies are
blooming in my irises

sprinkles of starlight are
gazing out from my pupils

octopus ink is
spilling from my throat

buttery honeysuckle vines are
growing in my marrow

slow dance circles are
dragging my chafed heels

dizzy

d   i   z   z   y

within these walls

a few thousand years ago,
sirens sang from cliffs
to sailors lost at sea

now they screech at me
because i've fallen from the cliff
and i have gotten lost at sea.

ania epul

walls.

i turn around,
and i still see walls

i want to run,
but i am trapped by halls

i try to end my life,
but i'm stopped by a mob

within these walls

maybe one day
when i'm living in a cardboard box
on the side of the street,
all the people who forced me to stay
will regret not letting me go.

labyrinthine thumbprints tattooed these windows
eggshell skulls pressed against these walls
eyeless sockets stared at these ceilings
swirls of hair carpeted these floors
ill intentions dangled from these door hinges
latex blue hands purpled this flesh

heartbeats hiccupped
stomachs churned
insides poured out
here.

~ wow.

within these walls

it's an unkind promise
a heartwarming lie
spoonfed sanity

rows and columns
grids in charts
nearby job listings

misunderstood undertakings
of valiant heroism,
having died down to the dull eddy of daily drowning

~ not here for the money

the springs on the doors make the same sound as this little girl
when she's running out of air
        deflating

i wake up from nightmares
of doors shutting,
their springs wheezing

and i always run to check if she's okay,
and i find her running out of air
in this waking nightmare

i call out for help, and the marble soldiers march in,
and they shut the doors and lock this little girl away,
but she's running out of air!

i see a sliver of her in the crack
my throat is closing
the springs on the doors are wheezing

all three of us are running out of air

within these walls

i pound on the walls to save her

please move!
i beg,
like my life depends on it,
with tears in my eyes
with desperation around my throat

but it doesn't budge
stares coldly back
with a hint of a smirk
on that face of distaste

i push and push at the walls,
and suddenly they're pushing me back

these walls—
they're human beings.

a witch's broomstick is growing out of her skull
electricity

so many hands trying to grip the handle
thunderstorm

tomato juice is everywhere
      everywhere

i can't believe she's only been on this planet
for ten years

those ten years must've felt like ten thousand
ten thousand years in an electric chair
ten thousand years soaking up the thunderstorm
ten thousand years with her mouth stuffed full of tomato
wedge

LET ME DIE!
she screams and screams,
and her voice makes the plate tectonics beneath us quiver
LET ME DIE LETMEDIELETMEDIE

i find myself suffering from paralysis
my skeleton is turning to stone
her voice makes the nerves inside me quiver
i am frozen inside.

i almost wanna say
just let her die!
she can't take it anymore.

within these walls

they teach us not to kill ourselves
by killing who we are

ania epul

it's a crime to cry around here
mudslide tears
running over my poppyseed nose
these grains of salt
scream their way down the drain

it's a crime to cry around here.

within these walls

where age isn't just a number,
but a qualification

where abilities don't restrain you,
but they'll be your jurisdiction

where your past doesn't define you,
but it's your certification.
it'll be your jurisdiction.
it becomes your qualification.

~ neglect subjectivity

ania epul

life isn't bad enough

it isn't bad
it isn't bad
life isn't bad

                              family

                      education

food

        electricity

              clothes

                                    government

                            healthcare

            running water

                                        technology

            roof

so why do i feel so abandoned
and starved

depleted.
cold.
lost.

sickdirtydisconnected

lying awake underneath the sky?

within these walls

here's to the all the suits and ties
who think it's as simple as
squeezing playdough

a toast to all the impassive faces who have devoted their lives
to locking and unlocking doors

a tip of my top hat to all the certificates
who believe ten days of order
is going to erase ten years of chaos

here's one *thundering*
round of applause.

lungs sheathed from smog
with a scabbard that smites the thrum in veins
the tick of heart
the itch of blackened fingers and diamond nails

that last
gleaming bead of
      bleeding salt

hold your breath
as the powdered plaster dwindles to dust
and the hairline cracks begin to gape like webs of canyon
beneath, they search for cyclones of cinder
curdles of decay

but instead, they find the tinkling echo of a spring
that once held
not a single
      grain of salt

~ unbound

within these walls

metal bars
velcro straps
iron fingers

needle
drugs

the world's getting blurry

the last thing i see is a huddle of stony-faced clowns,
but they're sitting there watching me like *i'm* the one wearing
the crimson nose,
as they chat and sip their coffees

i think i recognize those tomato wedges
feelingless parabolas
but i can't tell through this haze

who *are* you, you strangers!

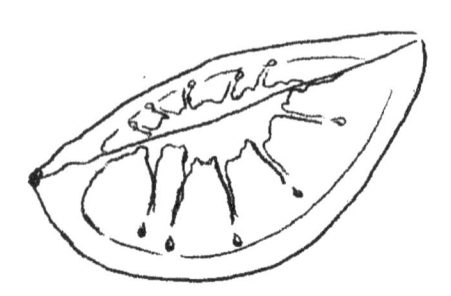

ania epul

fall asleep from a nightmare
into a nightmare

draw the curtains
and wake up to a nightmare

~ cycling

within these walls

what had begun as relief
quickly turned to horror,
but as time numbed the surprise,
all that was left was the day-to-day dread

i didn't sign up for this shit.
YOU HEAR ME?

i didn't sign up for this shit, I SAID

if i knew what i know now, i'd say no
i'd stay in the womb
i'd close my eyes and refuse to be born
i'd hold on tight and wait for the storm to be over
a storm that would never have started
if only i knew what i know now

shit
if i knew what i know now...

within these walls

all those people
who died when i didn't

good people
who wanted to live

and i wish i could've
just taken their place

jealous eyes
breathe no freedom,
but *your time will come*
your time will come

throats of knives
parch poisonous mouths,
but *your time will come*
your time will come

unlearned unconscious
hides faithful conscience,
but *your time will come*
your time will come

wooden limbs
creak beneath wooden smiles,
and i think to myself,
my time is.   not.   coming.

within these walls

some days i wonder if i'm meant to survive
if every breath is labor, why should i try?
even cut to pieces, i can barely get by
even with a head-full of meds, i'm still seeing in double
if i lie awake every night, is it even worth the trouble?

ania epul

i'm going in circles
no end, no beginning
different shades of shitty
different brands of insomnia
flavors of insecure

i'm going in circles
no end, no beginning

within these walls

if only you knew what was in there
dry-blood rust clinging to those circuits,
thick with the tang of sharp metal
cracked dirt like plaque on the wires
the old rag long since dried and hardened in the mouth of those sockets

i called in a technician to check it out,
and the moment he saw what was in there,
he told me something wasn't right
and i'd better find an electrician instead,
but the electrician said he'd never seen something so awry
and that place gave him the heebie-jeebies
and why don't i get the repairman
and the repairman directed me to the maintenance man
and the maintenance man gave me the engineer's number
and the engineer never picked up his phone

damn, when i called the technician,
i imagined myself leaving with a brand new set of gleaming circuits and wires,
but here i am, still sitting at the center of serpent coils and broken hardware,
trapped at the center of this sickly labyrinth

this place gives me the heebie-jeebies.

i wish i could leave too.

on the other side of the glass,
a man sips his coffee as he walks
a bus goes by and a woman gets off
a little boy bends over to tie his shoes

on this side of the glass,
a girl scratches her nose
a lock clicks and the doors open and close
a boy shuffles a deck seven times

we look at each other,
and nobody speaks

twenty drops of water drip from the mouth of the faucet
the hour hand on the clock inches on
the sky turns dark
paint dries

nobody speaks
but we sit together—
sit and stare.

~ languor

within these walls

like moths to a flame,
we flock to anyone
with a trace of fresh air
still lingering upon them

doesn't it just
take your breath away
to think what a commodity
fresh air has become?

ania epul

i wait as the seasons change
summer turns to stone
the next president is sworn into office
the little brothers and sisters are off to high school
my parents grow old
smiles wilt
gold castles fall to dusty shadows

the earth ventures around the sun,
time and time again

slowly, i am erased
the world has become a different place

and still, i wait.

~ within these walls

within these walls

where did i leave them
the clown nose
barred teethprinted smilemechanical limbs
where the hell did they go

when did they even disappear?

i can't believe it's all gathering dust in the back of some closet

i have to put this personality back on like a jacket
i have to put on a show

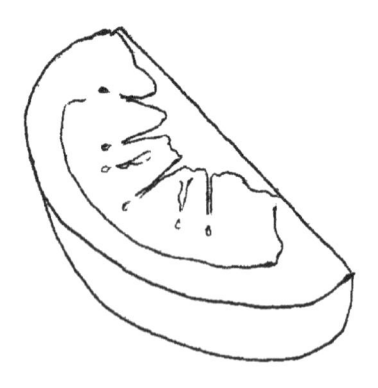

my life is meaningless, but if i just stay on
autopilot and keep filling up my schedule with a shit load of
nothing, then maybe i'll
use up all of my energy and the world just
spins and the
cracks in my skull
rust a little, but
it's okay, as long as i keep feigning
productivity, even though
this is a joke

~ who am i kidding

within these walls

wilt in the silence
stay awake in the dark
forget to speak
to cement your plaid heart

ania epul

it's ironic:
the less you say,
the happier they are

and when they're happy,
somehow, they think you are too.

within these walls

i deserve a round of applause
for being invincible

i shit you not
that i don't feel shit these days

test me
take a swing
say what you wanna say
do what you wanna do
turn my red nose blue

go ahead
shoot me with a bullet
        i won't even flinch

~ remember this?

ania epul

we know we're on our way out
because one by one,
we're shown the framed image
of the glass half empty,

and we're asked to say what we see
so one by one, we say,
half full!
half full, of course!

like a line of bots, we are set free
with our batteries plugged in and our joints greased
with our screws screwed tight and our circuits cleaned

half full, we say,
and that's four more ounces riding the train tracks down to her stomach
four more ounces that burns his throat

half full, we say
to the glass half full
that's brimming to the edge with dread
half full, we say to the glass
that to some, are better off half empty

four ounces
doused by the iced cold,
and just like that,
our sparks go out

within these walls

they keep you around
and waste your life
until they feel like you're becoming a waste of theirs,
and then they let you go.

i cried
when i walked out of those doors

because even the people who once chained you
will offer you embraces
when they know you'll be gone

because even people whom you've never seen smile
will wear broad grins
when they're celebrating your departure

well, let me just tell you,
i cried
when i walked out of those doors

~ tears of joy

within these walls

it's here. the golden hour.
H	Y	P	E

and it feels like nothing.

i am estranged from my memories
i am unempathetic toward my past

this must be a joke
the golden hour

did i really work my heart dry for

    this?

teeth clenched with the effort to keep going,
pouring sweat and tears,
and everyone thought these bared teeth were grinning

i wish i could broadcast the secret
and let go of the goddamn

    A	N	T	I	H	Y	P	E

there's still a backlight lit
behind these red velvet walls
i stand in the spotlight all alone
and grin to myself

because

                    wow.

i've done it

i've put on a show

but then i taste the red in my mouth,
and the cotton puff falls from my nose
i'm a popped water balloon
and suddenly, i'm sitting in a puddle all alone,
a silhouette underneath the spotlight

and

                    wow.

damn is it lonely
behind these red velvet walls

within these walls

finally got these claws on the pen
now i get to write the script
and pull these strings
and create the ending

but i can't fucking move or speak
i'm not writing this story
the story's writing me
propelling me onward
        onward toward the epilogue

ania epul

i can't tell what's worse:
not doing anything,
paralyzed by the memory of being this powerless,
or doing everything,
although i am utterly powerless

~ still

within these walls

i catch sight of a sliver of sky
before the metal doors slam shut

in the semidarkness,
i can hear my heart thumping in my chest

more than anything,
i feel betrayed

you promised you would stop,
i accuse

the heartbeats are laughter
pulsing in my throat

and you fell for it again!
they answer

ania epul

it's sort of a joke
because you fell for it too,
didn't you

you thought i was really made of rainbow yarn
and oversized shoes

that's why you're so surprised to be locking the doors on me again,
isn't it

well, read the damn manuscript
didn't you see this coming up in the epilogue?

oh, did you think the story ended at the epilogue?

no.

this is how it goes.

epilogue

you're sick and tired?
thisisajoke

I AM SICK AND TIRED

i had learned to trudge ahead with swallowed incredulity
and prod myself forward in defeated compliance
toward inevitable decay
    (which others refused to see)

when at last,
with adamant sincerity
and tentative untangling,
i was guided to a stop on my fruitless path
and steered in a different direction.

~ a miracle

within these walls

at new year's
we watched fireworks
instead of becoming them

and we resolved to be better people
instead of blaming each other
for not being good enough

~ new times

and one time,
we pulled over in the middle of the road
because it was snowing outside

i hadn't seen snow in so long
i'd forgotten what it looked like

white powder petals
caught on my eyelashes
and blurred out the world

i kept thinking,
if only things were like this all the time

if only the sharp-outlined world
could always be hidden by something as delicate
and as tiny as a flake of snow

within these walls

but i cannot do this

i cannot keep up this show

i cannot fill up this theater with the emptiness gnawing at my stomach
i cannot paint an illustrious backdrop with the eigengrau consuming my irises
i cannot grow a symphony from the ache in my marrow

i cannot play every role and every character
i *cannot* be phenomenal and extraordinary

i am tired and alone, and i never
wanted to just collapse into bed
so much
and go to sleep,
let go of the parabola

i cannot twirl and dance for this audience anymore!
i cannot!

but you don't have to, you said. *you don't have to CONQUER THE WORLD!*

all you have to do is wake up tomorrow.
and tomorrow, we will conquer tomorrow.

i'll always be in your corner.
you have me. okay?
i'm here for you.

i am still proud of you.
i am proud of you. no matter what.

c'mere
i care about you, okay?
don't forget that

there's something endearing about you,
and i think it's really hard for you to feel hope right now,
so until you're ready, i'll hold onto that hope for you.

i could never give up on you.
don't give up on yourself.

are you gonna be okay?
i'm gonna see you again, right?
you're gonna be okay.

i am rooting for you.
and so is the universe.

within these walls

when i was four years old,
my mother asked me,
what are you going to be in ten years?

fourteen,
i said
and shrugged my shoulders

on the last day of kindergarten,
the teacher asked everyone,
what will you be in ten years?

immortal,
i promised
and grinned a toothy grin

when i started middle school,
we were given a survey:
where do you see yourself in ten years?

rotting in the ground,
i thought,
but i wrote down *i don't know*

before you let me go yesterday,
you said,
maybe i'll see you in ten years

and i shrugged my shoulders
maybe, i said
and thought, *maybe i'll have become immortal,
or maybe i'll be rotting in the ground*

but maybe i'll just be twenty-five

this is where
i learned to smile without tearing my face
to laugh without hollowing my insides
to speak without gathering lies
to hear the words *i care*
without rolling my eyes

this is where
i learned to be human:
not fixed
and not perfect,
but a human who has not yet departed from life.

~ clean slate

within these walls

before i left,
i tried to thank you,
but you widened your eyes:
for what?

for being there with me.
for being there with me even when i wasn't.
for saving my life.

i didn't do anything! you said

you *did.*

but you were wrong.

i cried
when i walked out of those doors

not because people were shoving me out the door
with their forceful palms pretending to be gentle pats on the back
not because i knew i'd finally made it to the end of the dark tunnel
    (one of them at least)
and my relief was pouring out of me, palpable and wet

i cried
when i walked out of those doors

even though i could feel the warmth of smiles on my back,
and the echoes of your voices were still in my head

i just had this terrible feeling in my stomach,
like the déjà vu was already stirring
i think they call it premonition
i knew it all ended here

wanted. safe. cared for.

the lights at the end of the tunnel were flickering,
like those lamps in horror movies
right before something horrible happens

i cried
when i walked out of those doors

it's not that i didn't want to go
i just…

didn't want to go.

within these walls

the drive home is jarringly lonely.
it's just me, so i pick the music,
and no one complains
no one asks to change it

we pass by a drive thru
no one asks to stop

the windows fog up
no one graffities their name

we stop at a red light,
and no one yells hello at the guy puffing a cigarette in the front seat.
i almost want to, but the atmosphere's turning solid
the sound waves won't carry
my jaw is cemented shut

i'm in a different world now.

a dead silent world where there are no sweets
and no fog, just rain
and no art
and so many red lights that they burn the horizon,
but not a single person to say hello to.

~ hiraeth

there is no one back home
waiting for the return of No One

also,
there is no one back home
waiting for the return of me

i guess me and No One
are in the same boat

within these walls

i almost walk straight off the edge of the cliff,
expecting there to be ground
where there is not

but there is not,
so i find myself treading water,
and it doesn't take long before my arms are aching
and my legs are burning

my whole body is sore
my heart rate is through the roof
lactic acid is clogging my brain

and then it hits me:
why am i even trying to stay afloat?

ania epul

why, why, why did you let me go?
my palms were still sticky
the scabs weren't finished peeling
the bruises were still healing
i'm sorry i keep bleeding!

but i'm just wondering
why
why
why did you let me go?

within these walls

lead a soul
to the brink of life,
only to extinguish its

boundless infinities

the way you would
the butt
of a used cigarette

ania epul

in the background,
i am nothing but an ink spot,
so no one notices

in the foreground,
i am a pestering buzz,
so someone crushes me

lifeless, i am nothing but an ink stain
someone scrubs me off,
and i'm gone

~ housefly

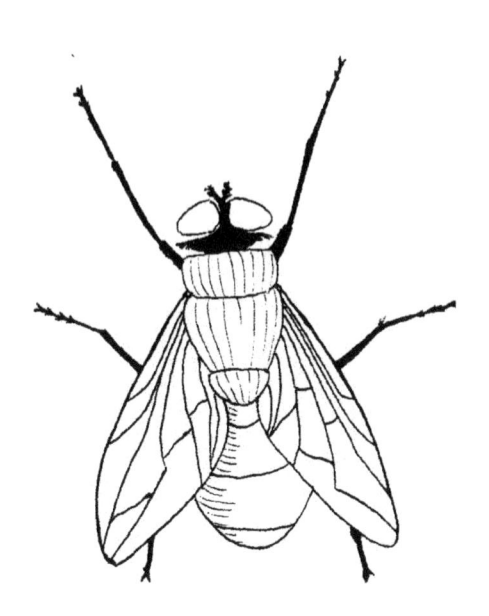

within these walls

you find pieces of other people inside you when you

stop
and stare

at the things you used to pass by unwittingly

you laugh at those things—
laugh until you cry

if ever i meant something to someone,
i don't now.

for years, i've been disappearing,
a tiny sailboat tossed by the sea
splintered to pieces, it floats astray

one shard of glacier
out in the deep
isolated from the ice caps, it melts away

one small island
in the middle of the ocean
unanchored, adrift, it's drowned by the rain

if ever i meant something to someone,
i've been long since replaced

i was told if i died,
it would be such a waste,
but it's already a waste

i've wasted away

i could never have meant anything
i can feel myself

~ fade

within these walls

why do i always wait
for the people who have left me forever
to come back?

what if i were a wonderful enough person
that i would never have to wait?

that people would never leave in the first place?

ania epul

what i don't understand
is how people can abandon you
without once turning back

and then they somehow expect you to live the rest of your life for them
just so they don't have to find out how it feels to be abandoned

within these walls

i'm the one who's striving to leave,
so why am i the one who's always getting left behind?

i still see your hard eyes in my mind,
still feel the bullets shoot off your tongue,
the lead sink into my skin

i still remember the tug on the corners of my lips
when you made me smile,
still hear the sound of your laugh

when i go, will i take all of our memories with me?
and away from you?

i'm the one who's reaching for the door,
but i would never shut it in your face
i'll be walking out the door,
but i'll never walk out of your life.

you did that.

just you wait.
the next time you see me, you'll be asking,
who are *you, you stranger?*

i've still got the facepaint and striped pants in my closet,
and i'm going to dig them out right now.

and i'll dump my insides out into a bucket
and shove it in the spot where the costume used to be

my fingers are getting black and blue
my lips are turning crimson
my nose is getting itchy
i can't breathe with this fucking cotton ball on my nose,
but i like it that way

who needs oxygen anyway?

within these walls

i almost forgot how good this feels

now i have clean insides
pristine
shrinking stomach
dead head

dying inside

~ ecstatic

ania epul

i'm not hungry
for human contact

i like the rusting corners
i like the dry rot climbing up the walls

i don't want to share my breath with you
i don't need you to speak to me

i live for the pit in my stomach
i exist for the starvation high

i'm not hungry
i'm stuffed with rusting corners
i am bloated with dry rot

within these walls

blank like pieces of printer paper
thrown on the floor

blank like the canvases
our laughter ignored

blank like the ocean
your little brother drew with fine tip pen

blank like their faces
when we were speaking in code

this page should be blank.

blank like my mind when
??? ? ? ? ?

ania epul

i should've called your phone or something
i remember i dialed your number recently,
but i didn't hit call
i don't know why

how could i have been so stupid?

isn't it crazy that i thought i knew what it felt like to be left behind?
now i know i didn't have a clue
isn't it crazy that i thought i would be the first
i don't know why

why was i so naïve?

i punch in your number now
this time, i hit call
i can't shake the feeling that you'll pick up
i don't know why

this is crazy.
this is crazy.
this is crazy.
i'm going crazy

within these walls

everything is behind me.
nothing is ahead.

everything that happened happened
everything that i dreamed of isn't coming
everything that was ever going to happen already came and went,
and it's too late to change any of it

nothing's coming anymore.
i've come so far,
just so i could stop here
and have no where to go

if i could go back,
i'd tell myself,
don't even bother showing up.

~ run out of road

ania epul

when we're gone,
a stranger will call us amazing
a classmate will say we were strong
those who left us will only then start to miss us,
as if that will bring us back

they'll say how they've always loved us
how they'll keep our memories alive
exclaim how important we were
insist that we changed their lives

but it's too late to say these words,
because we will never know.

if you care, show it
if you mean it, say it
say it when we're here to hear it

say it when we're here.

~ hear to here it

within these walls

i miss it.

sometimes, the echo makes me smile
out of the blue

cracks the rock that's hardened around me
a gentle trickle
a warm flood that tugs at me
and i begin to thaw

but then i remember
how i was such an idiot
and how you don't miss me
and how even if you did,
i would just wish you'd forget how stupid i was,
erase me from your mind

and then i remember
to be as cold as ice

do you ever stop short
in the middle of another one of your billion breaths

ask yourself
how it could possibly be
that you've gotten yourself into this mess

search yourself
for any reflection of the you
that you always thought you'd be

wonder in bewilderment
why no part of the you that you are
holds even a fragment of how you thought you'd turn out?

within these walls

i've done so many things that i hate myself for

and i'm sorry.

the only thing that helps is thinking that when i'm dead,
none of it will matter anymore,
that maybe you'll see the apology written on my casket,
and that'll overshadow everything i've done

and maybe you'll forgive me,
and in that moment, i'll finally be able to forget it all

that moment can't come soon enough

and *i'm sorry.*

it's easy to ignore the bad things,
and give yourself up
maybe the truth is too much.

maybe i am only fit for lies,
just like so many before me

maybe i deserve to die
believing in sunshine,
even though it's midnight

within these walls

i can't cry
when there are all those people out there suffering
their worlds are ending

i'd better keep in these alligator tears,
or else they'll wash away the blue triangles on my cheeks,
and then where would i be?

i can't laugh
when there are all those people out there gleaming
the world is theirs

i want to be like them,
but all i've got is the backdrop for company,
and there i was, thinking i was the star of the show.

ania epul

do you ever get too tired to talk
too exhausted to walk
too drained to sob
too empty to smile

so you lie down to go to sleep,
but you find that you're too tired for that too

within these walls

i woke up
and blinked

oKaY

that's enough for today!
let's not get ahead of ourselves now!

ania epul

she taps her fingers on her desk,
waiting for me to speak

i drum my knuckles on the table,
waiting for her to give up

we both wish it was over,
but neither of us moves.

~ say something

within these walls

you asked me if i wanted to get away
to a paradise of beautiful things

i told you that i'd love to,
but i can't because i'm afraid

i don't want to go far away
because what if you run way,
and the paradise loses its beauty,
and then i'm trapped in a nightmare
that you've led me into,
even if you didn't mean to

you said you won't,
so won't i go?
i said i'd love to,
but i can't.
there's nothing else i can afford to lose.

~ paradise

oh, don't you pry me open
don't you dig your nails into these clasps
you won't get your grimy fingers into the chasm of my mind

i have played this charade for millennia
i am the Bullshit Wizard
i am a Professional Con Artist

and you are giving me drapetomania
i hate the magnetism of your words
this stickiness

because i'm unhappy with nothing in my head
i know you know that this callow rainbow face is just a mirage

i know you know how lonely i am

i have erased every face i've ever seen
i've dehydrated every tear i've ever cried
i've wrung my mind until it's bone dry

i know you're looking for something,
but i won't let you pry me open.
don't you dig your nails into these clasps.
you won't get your grimy fingers into the chasm of my mind.

you don't know what's in there
it's better off left alone

i don't know what you think you'll find—
i don't remember.

within these walls

i read my old writings
and realized how many things
i forgot

remembered all the memories
i forgot

i can't believe just how much
i forgot

i wish they would stay
forgotten

because now i feel so
forgotten

before there was nothing,
there was something.

i don't remember much about her.

some people say we are like blocks of marble,
and life chips away at us as we grow,
sculpts us into who we are

i don't think that's true.
i think we are who we are—
arcadian diamond figurines

until we become blocks of marble
heartbeats frozen into stone
it grows like frost on our crystal lips
it glows like coal in our hollows

but my fingers feel soft now
why do i feel fissures spreading over my skin?
i think i'm becoming

~ talc

within these walls

she's draped in a black tissue this time
instead of the usual paper johnny

in her chest, there's a breathing, living being
quivering, quaking in that rib cage

it feels like a bulging lemon, constricted in a fist
it feels like all the little white seeds pouring out

it feels like the world is ending.

she doesn't know what to do
      how can this be happening
      howcanthisbehappening
      theworldmustbeending andeverythingmustgoaway

she closes her eyes
and shuts off the switches
pulls the plugs
saws through the wires

she is the Electrician.

no more of this.

the power's out now,
and in the dark,
she builds a stone tower around her soul

no one comes in.
and no one leaves.

~ seventeen

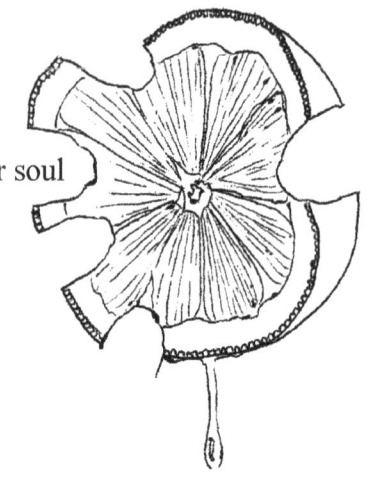

she's walking circles
in an infinite cathedral

there is no sky above us.
only a stone dome
with twelve gleaming teeth, clacking away
    tick tock

i don't know if they're grinning
or grimacing

she doesn't seem to notice.
the teeth are irrelevant to her

she only sees the cathedral.
it is her prison.

i'd say, *go for the doors and windows*
but there are no doors or windows
in this infinite cathedral

~ sixteen

within these walls

she found a family that year.

it was the best and worst thing in the world.

you see,
when you are suddenly given everything,
it's like a drug

you don't know what to do with all this luxury
it's screaming your name, but you can't tell if it's screaming for you
or screaming *at* you

you want to take it, but how can you?
what if you lose it?
better not risk it

but how can you pass up all *this*
maybe you should just try it
but no, you can't give yourself up to these strangers

it was all so confusing for her!

she spent the whole time fighting to keep what she was afraid even to have,
holding on so tight to the same people she was thrusting away

i wish she'd known all this sooner
and soaked it up while it lasted.
i wish she could've *just let go* of that tomato wedge

she found herself that year.
found. and then lost again.

~ fifteen

she will fight you to the very end.
oh, so you think the sky is blue?
there is no fucking way. it's red. ***it's red,*** i say!

you think you can get through to her?
don't kid yourself.
you can't.

keep hammering with that pickaxe.
she'll sit at the top of the mines and watch you
and laugh and laugh

after all, that's what clowns do, isn't it?

~ fourteen

within these walls

there was a set of train tracks
leading to the heart of an exploding tornado
growing out of a black hole
swirling in the midst of dying stars

we should've seen it coming
because we've been hurtling to this destination since the very beginning

but nobody said a word.
maybe they didn't notice.
maybe they didn't care.

she sat with her forehead pressed against the window,
watching as the plate tectonics quivered
and heat waves shivered
and molten lava bubbled
and cracks grew in the ground beneath our feet

and we sat in those red felt seats in the audience,
nodding to the rhythm of the dying heartbeat
humming to the silence
watching her hurtling to her destination

~ thirteen

petty thief
steals a bit everywhere she goes
snags something here and there

she keeps a collection
i think they're souvenirs

the silver hits the cutting board,
and tomato juice wells up and out
you'd think she'd take the balsamic to dress up her wounds,
but she takes a gleaming red wedge.

she doesn't think anyone sees her,
but i do.

i catch her every time.

the time she slipped the stoplight into her pocket
two diamonds from the jewelry store
a shield for her heart
some cotton for her head

~ twelve

within these walls

one day, the world stopped existing.

there was the horizon touching the sea
there were the infinite mites, crawling the green carpets

so how did i know the world had stopped existing?

because i clamped my hands over my ears
and squeezed my eyes shut,
waiting for her to pull the trigger,
bullets kissing bullets
      (first line of defense is always offense)
but nothing came.

it was dead silent.

i opened my eyes and looked around for her,
but she was gone.

in a manner of speaking.

her eyes were the haze clinging to the horizon,
her tears the sea
a million fiery ants crawled up and down her spine and clawed
at her insides,
but she was merely part of the scenery

to her, the world had stopped existing.

~ eleven

before her closet was stuffed full with costumes,
corsets of lies and jackets of personalities,
it was filled with white collared shirts and khaki pants

and a backpack.

inside, there were three water bottles
a wad of cash
ten bars of chocolate
and her favorite pair of jeans

the backpack was always growing.
we had to stock up for disaster,
so when the hurricane hit, we'd be ready to run

but the hurricane was always hitting,
so we were always packing our bags

everything that disappeared into that bag was a declaration
of independence
a letter of goodbye
an envelop of dreams

i am running away from this nightmare! they screamed
and i'm not coming back!

but she always did.
after all, how much can ten bars of chocolate withstand?

~ ten

within these walls

we lived in a magical land.

there, the walls could talk,
and they jabbered away at us, so we'd never have to be alone
we spent hours in front of those walls,
sharing our secrets
telling each other jokes
keeping each other company

in this magical land, the sun never set,
and we stayed up under the lamplight,
withstanding the nightmares together
braving all of the battles
brandishing our swords until our arms were sore

gods and goddesses were watching over us,
and if we were ever in trouble,
they'd answer us.
i believed it with all my heart.

but just in case they don't,
tell the walls i say goodbye,
and i will miss them,
and thank you for standing by me when no one else did.

~ nine

within these walls

i wanted a rainbow freeze pop from the ice cream truck,
the kind with the bubble gum hidden at the bottom.

i wanted gel pens for my colorings books
and to be first to the tire swing at recess
and to get my cast off because it was so itchy
and a new composition notebook for every new idea i had
and to go to someone's birthday party
and to have a few friends at school

and for my parents to hear me crying at night, so they'd come
get me and i wouldn't have to be alone
and for the nightmares to go away
and someone to talk to, someone to confide in, someone to
understand me
and to feel safe and wanted for once

and i wanted to die because the universe was too big
and i was too small
and i was running out of time
and everyone i loved was dying
and i couldn't stand being trapped in these arms and legs,
imprisoned within these walls

and i regretted everything i'd ever done
and i was terrified of all the hour hands turning
and i didn't want to get out of bed in the mornings
and i was so overwhelmed and scared and lonely
and i didn't enjoy anything
and i didn't know what the meaning of it all was
and i just didn't know what to do anymore

i wanted a polyester bunny with super long ears,
the kind that stays soft,
even if your mom accidentally puts it through the wash.

~ wanting for nothing

ania epul

i am afraid of the unknown.

but knowing makes me afraid.

within these walls

oh my.

i didn't realize.

i didn't recognize her

i didn't recognize
myself

without that red nose
without her freshly cut tomato wedge
and wire eyelashes
those signature blue slices, growing out of her eyes

i'm scared.
i don't want this to be true.
i am not her, am i?

i check my reflection in the camera lens
       (they've got one set up for the show)

i expect to see my cotton crimson nose
my perfectly carved rose parabola
my luscious black fan
my phthalo isosceles

but instead, i see her.
i see **her.**

for years,
i drained my time.

my only condolence
was that i would be my own keeper of time

little else mattered.
unwittingly, i was sucked away
by all of the inconsequential stories

and when i looked around,
i'd lost sight of the flame
tended to by the self i was at four

for years,
i drained my time
trying to drain my life

my only condolence
is that i will be my own keeper of time.

~ purpose

within these walls

i wonder if ten years from now,
looking back
will mean that people are remembering the person i was,
thinking of all the unspoken things that were there when i was there too,
discovering all of the things that i've left behind.

or if they'll marvel at how much i've changed,
and they'll be reading my words
and listening to my melody
and even though in that case, i'm really dead to them too,
i won't be dead to the world
they'll remember the person that i was when i was in their lives,
and smile because *i've made it*.

or maybe they'll shake their heads at how much i've changed,
and they'll be looking at me with curious eyes,
while i stare at them with blank ones
and they'll bring up the things that we laughed about when we were there together
when i've long since forgotten
how to laugh.

but really,
ten years from now,
i'll probably be sitting around
and they'll be sitting around,
and we'll both be sitting in little alcoves of the world,
but we won't be sitting together.

and then,
will anything really have changed at all?

~ retrospect

Lightning Source UK Ltd.
Milton Keynes UK
UKHW010046170223
417092UK00012B/677/J